THE TEDDY BEAR HISTORY OF THE WORLD

Born in Germany in 1905, Bruno Bruin, who comes from the distinguished Steiff family, moved to Britain as a young bear. He is currently cartoonist-in-residence at the national Teddy Bear Museum in Stratford-upon-Avon. This is his first book. Its sequel, the *Encyclopedia Beartannica,* is currently in preparation.

THE TEDDY BEAR HISTORY OF THE WORLD

Bruno Bruin

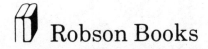
Robson Books

The Teddy Bear History of the World would not have been possible without the help and inspiration of my friend and collaborator Michael Buckner. It is to him, the best kind of human, that this book is dedicated.

B.B.

First published in Great Britain in 1989 by Robson Books Ltd, Bolsover House, 5–6 Clipstone Street, London W1P 7EB

British Library Cataloguing in Publication Data
Bruin, Bruno
  The teddy bear history of the world.
  1. English humorous cartoons-collections
  I. Title
  741.5'942

ISBN 0 86051 610 5

Printed in Great Britain by
St Edmundsbury Press Ltd, Bury St Edmunds, Suffolk

CONTENTS

**'Never in the field of human conflict
has so much been owed by so many
to so few.'**

On 20 August 1940 the British Prime Minister
Winston Churchill used those words in his tribute
to those who fought in the Battle of Britain. The
same could be said perhaps of the silent army of
teddy bears that has conquered hearts across
the world. Have you ever stopped to wonder
what might have happened if the teddy bear
had arrived with the Creation? It could have
changed the whole story of the planet earth and
have given us....

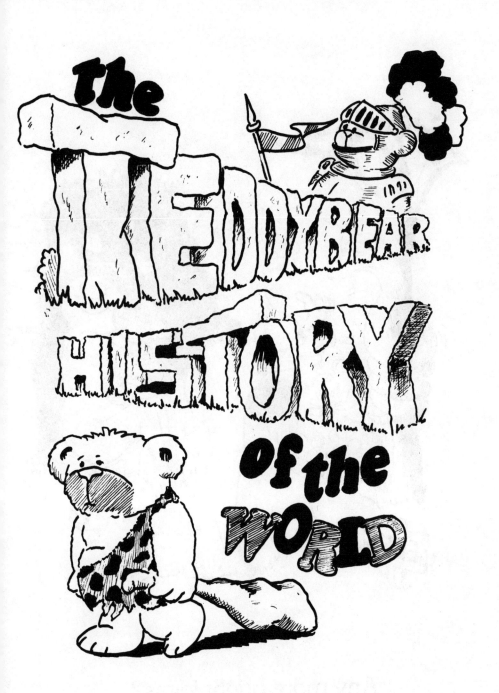

Any more bright ideas?

If you ask me, I think it's going to look damn silly in the history books.

Et tu Bruno?

Remember the good old days
when they used to quake with
fear at the sight of our
figurehead?

Speak to me Harold.

Kiss me Teddy!

No one does that to my teddy
bear and gets away with it!

Dr Livingstone, I presume?

1940 — The **Bear**litz

1953 — **Ted**mund Hillary
conquers Everest

One small step for man, one
giant step for mankind.

The Teddy Bear HALL OF FAME

Ben**fur**

Bearwulf

Beardicea

Ro**bear**t Bruce

Christofur Columbus

Anne **Bear**leyn

William Shakes**bear**

But hark what light at yonder
window breaks? It is a teddy
bear!

Alas poor teddy!

Napoleon **Bear**naparte

Bear Brummell

William Wil**bear**force

Ted Kelly

Buf**fur**lo Bill

Wild **Bear** Hickock

John Logie **Bear**

Lawrence of Ara**bear**

Albear**t** Einstein

Christiaan **Bear**nard

LEGENDARY BEARS

Excali**bear**

Ro**bear**son Crusoe

'The bears, the bears!' The
Hunch**bear** of Notre Dame

Peter **Panda**

Judge **Ted**

Bears from the worlds of music, the
movies, television and sport

Bearthoven

Dame Nelly Mel**bear**

Sir John **Bear**birolli

Li**bear**ace

Chuck **Bear**y

Beary Manilow

Humphrey **Bear**gart

Ted Astaire

Christo**fur** Lee

Colum*bear*

Bearny Hill

Bruce **Fur**syth

David **Bear**llamy

David Atten**bear**

Beary Whitehouse

Ian **Bear**tham

George **Bear**st

Frank **Bruno**

Severiano **Bear**lesteros

BEARS
OF THE
FAMOUS

Baden-Powell's bear

Prince Charles's bear

Agatha Christie's bear

Jacques Cousteau's bear

Noel Coward's bear

Roald Dahl's bear ... A Tale of the
Unexpec**ted**

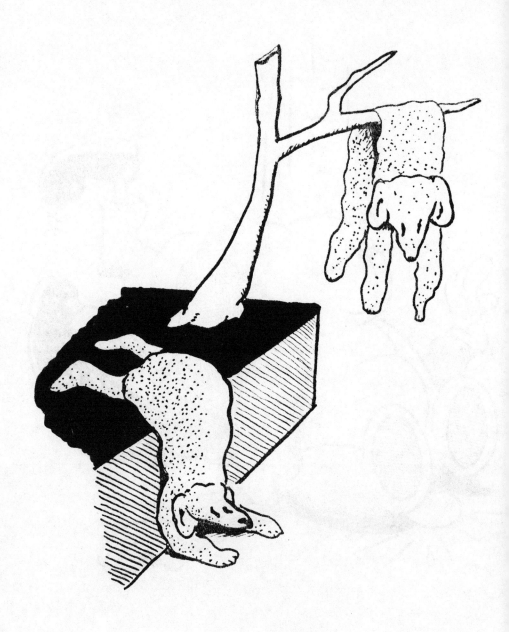

Salvador Dali's bears

Sir Arthur Conan Doyle's bear

Count Dracula's bear

Vincent Van Gogh's bear

Rolf Harris's bear

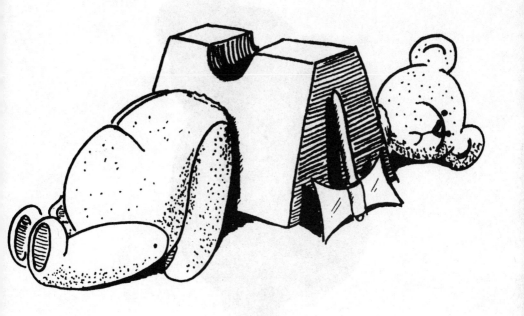

Henry VIII's bear

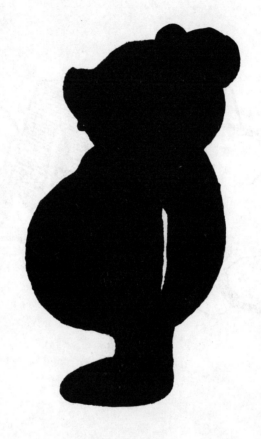

Alfred Hitchcock's bear

Houdini's bear

Patrick Moore's bear

Rupert Murdoch's bear

Picasso's bear

Mary Shelley's bear

Steven Spielberg's bear

William Tell's bear

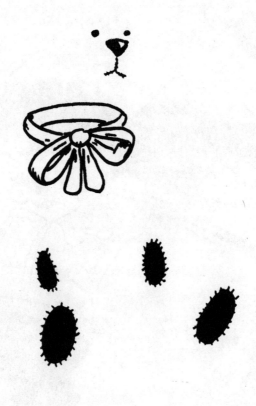

H G Wells's bear

BEAR FACTS

HOW TEDDY GOT HIS NAME

The teddy bear owes his name to President Theodore 'Teddy' Roosevelt, twenty-fifth President of the United States. On 14 November 1902 Roosevelt was on a hunting expedition in Smedes, Mississippi. Anxious that the President bag a bear, some of his party chased down and stunned a 235 lb black bear. The hunters roped the animal and tied it to a tree. A messenger was dispatched to summon the President so that he might shoot the bear and go home with a trophy. When Roosevelt arrived, he declined to shoot the tethered creature and, in suitably presidential tones, declared: 'Spare the bear!' The next day *The Washington Post* informed the nation: 'President called after the beast had been lassoed, but he refused to make an unsportsmanlike shot.' A cartoonist, Clifford Berryman, immortalized this moment in a drawing for *The Washington Post* and soon after the incident the President was approached by a shopkeeper from Brooklyn called Morris Michtom who sought permission from the White House to manufacture a small toy bear-cub and be allowed to call it 'Teddy's Bear'. The rest, as humans say, is history....

WHO MADE THE FIRST TEDDY BEAR?

Despite the claims of Morris Michtom, in Germany they credit the invention of the teddy bear to the Steiff company, which was begun at Giengen in Swabia in 1880 by a crippled seamstress called Margarete Steiff. The business began as a home workshop producing felt elephants but, by 1902, Steiff were manufacturing a wide range of soft toys, including cats, dogs, pigs, donkeys, horses and camels but not, until 1903, a bear. Bruno Bruin is a Steiff bear and dates from 1905, making him one of the oldest and most valuable bears in the world today. At auction it is invariably the early Steiff bears that fetch the highest prices. At Sotheby's in 1987, for example, a Steiff teddy from around

1904 fetched £5,720 and another Steiff from around 1913 was sold for the record sum of £8,800.

Britain's oldest teddy bear company is Dean's Rag Book Company who have been making teddy bears since around 1905. Chiltern Toys and Chad Valley are another two of the oldest names in the British toy industry and both firms began to produce bears around 1915. In 1967 Chiltern was taken over by Chad Valley and in 1978 Chad Valley was taken over by Palitoy. Merrythought of Ironbridge in Shropshire have been making bears since 1930 and their bears are easily recognizable, thanks to the distinctive label sewn on the footpad. Early Merrythought bears also featured a stud in one ear, not to be confused with the famous 'button in the ear' (in German, *Knopf im Ohr*), which is the hallmark of Steiff bears.

TEN FAMOUS BEARS AND THEIR CREATORS

In a recent survey people of all ages were asked to name famous teddy bears. Bears like Baloo and Yogi Bear were excluded because, even in cartoon form, they are intended to be real bears rather than teddy bears. Some people may feel that the same could be said of one or two of the bears on this list. Certainly, devotees of Rupert Bear would deny that he is or ever has been a teddy bear. They regard him as a unique phenomenon: a boy with a bear's head!

1 **Winnie the Pooh** created by A A Milne
2 **Rupert Bear** created by Mary Tourtel
3 **Paddington Bear** created by Michael Bond
4 **Sooty** created by Harry Corbett
5 **Fozzie Bear** created by Jim Henson
6 **Teddy Robinson** created by Joan Robinson
7 **Super Ted** created by Mike Young
8 **Tough Ted** created by Simon Bond
9 **Nookie Bear** created by Roger de Courcey
10 **Odd** created by James Roose-Evans

TEN FAMOUS TEDDY BEAR OWNERS

Archibald Ormsby-Gore
owned by **Sir John Betjeman**
Bear'd Dog
owned by **Elvis Presley**
Clarence Chair-Bear
owned by the **Marquess of Bath**
Delicatessen
owned by **Peter Bull**
  (Delicatessen played the part of Aloysius in the celebrated
  television version of Evelyn Waugh's novel *Brideshead
  Revisited*)
Humphrey
owned by **Margaret Thatcher**
Islwyn
owned by **Neil Kinnock**
Lady Elizabeth
owned by **HM The Queen Mother**
Mr Woppit
owned by **Donald Campbell**
Teddy
owned by **HRH The Prince of Wales**
The Prince of Love
owned by **Barbara Cartland**

THE TEDDY BEAR MUSEUM

The world's largest and finest collection of teddy bears can
be seen at Britain's Teddy Bear Museum in Stratford-upon-
Avon. Founded by Gyles and Michele Brandreth in 1987,
the Museum is set in an Elizabethan house in the heart of
Stratford, a stone's throw from the birthplace of William
Shakespeare (or was it William Shakesbear?). The Museum
is the home for hundreds of bears from over 20 countries,
including many of the oldest and most valuable in
existence. There are musical bears and mechanical bears,
large bears (including one that is 15ft tall!) and tiny bears
(including one that is smaller than a thumbnail), bears of
the famous and famous bears – among them the original
TV Sooty, the original Fozzie Bear, Peter Bull's Delicatessen
and, of course, the present author, Bruno Bruin.